Healing In His Wings:
How I Am Making It Through

Licia Johnson

WESTBOW
P R E S S®
A DIVISION OF THOMAS NELSON
& ZONDERVAN

This book is a work of non-fiction. Unless otherwise noted, the author and the publisher make no explicit guarantees as to the accuracy of the information contained in this book and in some cases, names of people and places have been altered to protect their privacy.

WestBow Press books may be ordered through booksellers or by contacting:

WestBow Press
A Division of Thomas Nelson & Zondervan
1663 Liberty Drive
Bloomington, IN 47403
www.westbowpress.com
844-714-3454

Because of the dynamic nature of the Internet, any web addresses or links contained in this book may have changed since publication and may no longer be valid. The views expressed in this work are solely those of the author and do not necessarily reflect the views of the publisher, and the publisher hereby disclaims any responsibility for them.

Any people depicted in stock imagery provided by Getty Images are models, and such images are being used for illustrative purposes only. Certain stock imagery © Getty Images.

Scripture taken from the King James Version of the Bible.

Scripture taken from the Amplified Bible, Copyright © 1954, 1958, 1962, 1964, 1965, 1987 by The Lockman Foundation. Used with permission.

ISBN: 978-1-6642-3500-7 (sc)
ISBN: 978 1-6642-3499-4 (hc)
ISBN: 978-1-6642-3501-4 (e)

Library of Congress Control Number: 2021910585

Print information available on the last page.

WestBow Press rev. date: 06/09/2021

Introduction

As one who loves to write and to express myself, I've always had the desire to write a short story about an experience of mine or just to see my name in bold letters: Staff Writer Licia Johnson. I did an internship for *The Daily Videte* at Illinois State University, and it was okay. When God told me to write this book, I was disobedient. I heard him clear as a bell and ignored him. It was like God came to me at a bad time. Eventually something within gave in, and I told God okay. Now, looking back, I wish I had taken that time seriously to ask God specific questions about the book he wanted me to write. Sexual abuse and molestation is a subject people don't want to talk about. While on my Christian journey, the Lord has placed people in my path to show me to not be afraid and to tell stories of young people who have suffered. This story is about one girl God has kept through all her pain and confusion. She has learned that God has not given us the spirit of fear, but of love, power, and of a sound mind (2 Timothy 1:7).

I want this book to be a blessing that will cause healing to go forth. There are so many people who are suffering right now with keeping secrets of abuse. God is saying it is time for all of His children who have suffered to be healed and delivered. No more shackles or chains! It is time for people to be set free and free indeed!

After preparing, researching, and praying while writing the book *Strength to Speak: One Woman's Struggle to Make Peace with Her Past,* Joy was initially relieved. "Yes. I have spoken, and now I no longer have to talk about this anymore. All is well." So she began to look for other subjects to write about. During this process, God showed her visions of speaking to large groups of people, and it frightened her. You might ask, "Why was she sacred?" Joy has a bad habit of making something small into a huge mountain. She allows the little things to overwhelm her. "How do I start making speeches? Whom will I speak to, or where will I go? I need someone to help me and lead the way. I am definitely not a leader. What if schools, churches, and organizations say no? Then what's the next step? But what I am now realizing is that I have to pray and have faith and the Lord will provide. And that's exactly what I plan to do."

Joy remembers vividly working at the bank and how her coworkers were excited when they found out she had written her first book, *Strength to Speak.* "Wow, Joy. You might become famous. Don't forget to sign my book; your signature might be worth millions."

Along this journey, the Lord has blessed Joy with a wonderful sister friend, Johanna, who is also a published author. During their friendship, Johanna continues to bless Joy by praying, guiding, and speaking life to her. She is the older sister Joy always wanted. Johanna insisted that this book was needed and that Joy had to start as soon as possible.

In actuality, there are two reasons why Joy stalled with moving forward. First, she just didn't want to do it. Second, she didn't really know what to write, and most of the time, she didn't feel like it; she was tired or not feeling well. Joy had to pray, seek God, shake the dust off her pen, and set her mind on things above. Sharing your own dark secrets to the world can be terrifying; however, Joy realized that she was not alone. At every book event she had, there was always one woman who experienced something similar. That would always give her hope to continue. Sometimes Joy would watch potential customers pass by at the literary fest. They would quietly examine the book from afar and walk away. It was sometimes disheartening to see. A large percentage of people did not want to read about that topic, and as of today, it's okay and she understands.

After Joy climbed the mountain of distributing the struggles of her life, she felt brand new. She thought, *Now I am ready to focus on my career and start dating.* Society says if you are single, something is wrong. The single life is lonely, broken, and boring, and getting married will fix it. Joy believed that lie, and it led her down a very dangerous path.

Being obsessed with love relationships and the desire to be married caused Joy to seek romantic relationships with men who were not available or interested. She was very thirsty, and it caused extreme embarrassment and hurtful disappointments. Even as a Christian woman, she was still looking for love from a man to make her feel complete or even healed from it all. Wrong! God is the true healer and deliverer. Matthew 6:33 (KJV) says, "But seek ye first the kingdom of God, and his righteousness; and all these things shall be added unto you."

Opening up the door to love relationships is dangerous, especially if you are not completely healed from your past. Joy found herself being transformed by the likes of the world, including attention, sex, love, or lust from the wrong men. Her Christian values were forgotten as she took on a new identity of no longer being a virgin. She started to sin on purpose, and this was hazardous to her relationship with Jesus Christ. She had to recommit her life to God and start over.

She said, "Lord, I am so ashamed. Please forgive me of my sins. I am sorry that I forgot about you and put the men in my life first. From now on, you will be first and foremost in my life."

She had to make some hard decisions. Prior to her dating, she was aware of sexual activity causing confusion that would definitely lead her astray. But her flesh enjoyed it all. Romans 7:19–20 (AMP) says,

> For the good that I want to do, I do not do, but I practice the very evil that I do not want. But if I am doing the very thing I do not want to do, I am no longer the one doing it [that is, it is not me that acts.] but the sin [nature] which lives in me.

She had to learn the hard way with experience being the best teacher.

She made the decision to be sexually active, and it hurt her in the long run. She gave her body for love, and the men she dealt with took it. They thought about marrying her, but that was it—just a thought. As one friend told her, "Don't set yourself up for failure. I never invite men over to my house—*ever*. We go out on a date for dinner, and then we go our separate ways. No need for either one of us to visit each other." And Joy did the opposite.

She now knows for sure the best person to be in love with is Jesus! He always gives an everlasting love. His love is honest and true. He will never lie, leave you, or forsake you.

He is always committed and faithful. His delays in life are planned *just for you* because he is the beginning and the end, the Alpha and the Omega. Remember it is okay to be single. Living the single life allows you to dedicate all your time to your Heavenly Father. Once you get involved in a relationship, that time is divided. You have to make every effort to put God first. Philippians 4:6–7 (AMP) says,

> Do not be anxious or worried about anything, but in everything [every circumstance and situation] by prayer and petition with thanksgiving, continue to make your [specific] requests know to God. And the peace of God [peace which reassures the heart, that peace] which transcends all understanding, [that peace which] stands guard over your hearts and your minds in Christ Jesus [is yours].

Stop rushing to date. Take time to be by yourself and figure out who you are and what you want to do with your life. Most importantly, focus on your relationship with Jesus.

Joy is a worrywart. Did you know that worrying is a sin? First John 4:18 (KJV) says, "There is no fear in love; but perfect love casteth out fear: because fear hath torment. He that fearth is not made perfect in love." Joy has always been anxious about the unknown, but as a Christian, she had to continue to put God first and meditate on his word.

Joy has been walking with the Lord for over twenty years, and she talks to him about everything. Why is it that she still struggles with her emotions and anxiety? She thought she was giving him all her problems and thoughts, but maybe not. She goes through the cycle of a day, and by the end of it, she feels better. How can she not allow her emotions to take her there again? She gets excited about a new year, job, and fresh beginnings, but along the way, that excitement turns into extreme nervousness. She displays symptoms of a queasy stomach and no appetite. She is not motivated to do anything. But as the cycle ends, she comes back to herself and relaxes. Her Christian coach told her to start saying positive affirmations daily like "I am always in the right place at the right time to receive the right information regarding advancement over my life." Or one that really should help her is "I am bold, beautiful, fierce, and confident. I will not allow anyone from my past, present, or future to intimidate me."

We should always hide scripture in our hearts to help us along the way. Second Timothy 1:7 (AMP) says,

> For God did not give us a spirit of timidity or
> cowardice or fear, but (He has given us a spirit
> of power and of love and of a sound judgment

and personal discipline (abilities that result in a calm, well-balanced mind and self-control).

She has to remind herself of this daily. She cannot get sidetracked and be in her own world of sadness and tears.

The Lord continues to confirm Joy with her purpose of writing and inspiring others with her life stories. One person responded, "My daughter, Chloe, enjoyed your book *Strength to Speak*. Thank you so much. Chloe had a similar experience, and reading your book allowed us to have a discussion about it." So God is showing Joy that her story matters because it has been helping women one by one. The lady was concerned about Joy. She asked her, "How are you doing now? Are you okay?" Joy quickly answered that she was fine, not really being honest. Then she thought about it. How would she explain to this lady that she really didn't know? Joy realized she needs to share her struggles with others so everyone can be free together, including herself.

Holding on to a traumatic event played a part in her struggles with anxiety. She was on the road to being whole again but would have a relapse. A good habit to start is to journal every day. Journaling is a great way to express your feelings and to recall things that happen daily.

As Joy was figuring out how to stop and slow down her anxiety, she discovered a few tips along the way.

- Breathing techniques. How often do you take a break from your hectic day, close your eyes, and inhale and exhale? Do it three times throughout the day. Are you upset about some bad decisions you made? Those decisions cause suffering, frustrations, and uncontrollable tears. Begin to take deep breaths and relax.

- Limit alcohol and caffeine. A vast majority of Americans start the day with a cup of coffee. A portion of our foods and beverages have caffeine, which tastes good and gives you the uptick you need. However, those with anxiety should avoid alcohol and caffeine as much as possible. Everything we put in our bodies will have a positive or negative effect. Choose to be wise and healthy.

- Exercise. When you are stressed, how do you deal with it? Change your environment or go outside and take a walk. We all need to do some cardiovascular exercise and keep moving. Being outdoors can magically calm the mind.

- Give yourself the proper nutrition. Today we know that anxiety is the result of constant chatter between different brain regions, a fear network. The world we live in is frightening, so we need to be careful what we watch, listen to, and say. Proverbs 18:21 (KJV) says, "Death and life are in the power of the tongue: and they that love it shall eat the fruit thereof." If you constantly say, "I am sick," you will become sick. But if you change it and say, "I am healthy and strong," that's what you become, and you have to believe it. You also have to be mindful of eating a healthy diet full of greens, vegetables, lean meats, fruit, and plenty of water.

The most important thing is to realize if *you* can't do it—heal on your own—remember God can do anything. Nothing is too hard for him, and sometimes as humans we forget that he is all-powerful!

Today Joy recognizes with help from her good friend that this is a ministry for her to empower women from the ages of four to twenty-five.

What are the seven steps she took to receive healing?

1. Tell your story to someone you trust and who can pray you through it. Getting help from other believers is uplifting.

2. Get therapy from a professional. Find a counselor, mentor, or good friend, and talk about it in detail. This is your time to release it and to cry. You will feel better. Start journaling your thoughts and paying attention to what you are thinking. Learn and memorize scripture. For every negative thought, come back with a scripture to lift you up. For example, if you are thinking *I'm scared*, remember God has not given you the spirit of fear but of love power and a sound mind.

3. Write a story, song, or poem, or maybe even draw a picture to express what you went through. Find inspirational music that talks about the love and power of God. Gospel music has the amazing power to lift up your spirit.

4. Find a church that will help you grow spiritually and gain strength from the Lord.

5. Learn how to seek God. Learn how to pray, praise, and worship. Immediately the enemy will flee, and the atmosphere will lighten and change. You will

start singing Johnny Nash's song lyrics "I can see clearly now the rain is gone!"

6. Seek your purpose or calling in life. Sometimes purpose is born out of a tragedy. Do your research; find books speaking on those particular things. Ask the Lord to show you what you were born to do. Also take into consideration your strengths, weaknesses, and activities you enjoy.

7. If possible, confront your perpetrator and forgive them; reach out and help someone else along the way. Challenging your perpetrator might be the most difficult thing you do. As you prepare to do it, it will help you stare the trauma you have experienced in the face and hopefully move on. If it is too difficult for you to square up to them, the next best thing is to go to God in prayer. Yes, Joy will never forget what happened, but in order for her to move forward and to be free, forgiveness is needed. Put all of it in God's hands.

Research conducted by the "Centers for Disease Control (CDC) estimates that approximately one in six boys and one in four girls are sexually abused before the age of eighteen. According to the US Department of Justice (nsopw.org), only

10 percent of perpetrators were strangers to the children and 23 percent of the perpetrators were *children* themselves!"

The following are nine things that could help your child be less vulnerable to sexual abuse:

1. "Talk about body parts early. Use proper names, such as vagina or penis. You should be able to comfortably discuss using these words with your child. This will benefit your child if something inappropriate happens.

2. Teach them some body parts are private. Only Mommy, Daddy, and the doctor should see them with their clothes off. People outside of the home should see them with their clothes on.

3. Teach your child body boundaries. Tell your child that no one should touch their private parts or ask them to touch somebody else's private parts.

4. Tell your child that body secrets are not OK. They should always tell you if someone tries to make them keep a body secret.

5. Tell your child that no one should take pictures of their private parts. Pedophiles love to take and trade

pictures of naked children. Tell your kids that no one should ever take pictures of their private parts.

6. Tell your child how to get out of scary or uncomfortable situations. Some kids might be uncomfortable telling an adult 'no' or that they have to leave and go potty.

7. Tell your child they will never be in trouble if they tell you a body secret. Tell your child they can always come to you and talk about body safety or body secrets.

8. Tell your child that a body touch might tickle or feel good. It is best to use the term "secret touch" so there will not be any confusion.

9. Tell your child that these rules apply even with people they know and even with another child. Explain to them that Mommy and Daddy can touch their body parts while bathing but no one else should touch them there. Not friends, aunts, uncles, teachers, or coaches.

Incorporate these talks while bathing your child or when they are running around naked. I believe if parents take the time to have these conversations with their children, and follow these rules, it's possible to catch some inappropriate things if they occur." 1

In conclusion, we have a Savior who died for our sins, and he is there waiting to hear from us on a daily basis. This Christian journey is never easy. You are going to have some wonderful memories. And on the other hand, you will have to fight for your life to be victorious. Just remember Jesus will be right by your side while leading you in the right direction.

Bibliography

Ten Ways to teach your child the skills to prevent Sexual Abuse: Straight talk about body parts and a no secrets policy can protect young kids without scaring them.

https://www.childmind.org

STRENGTH TO SPEAK

one woman's struggle to make peace with her past

Acknowledgments

I would like to thank God for the visionary, the Emeritus Bishop Arthur M. Brazier and his teaching on God's grace and mercy. And I thank my pastor, Dr. Byron Brazier, for his teaching on identity, character, and vision. I also thank God for the Holy Spirit. During the process of me writing this book, I fought against my fears, and whenever I attended the Day Timers, Dr. Brazier spoke to my situation every time and I thank him for that.

Dr. Catherine Gross and "Girl Can We Talk?," thank you for this ministry. It has truly changed my life. I don't know where I would be without the foundation of God's people.

Rev. Kay Robinson, may God continue to bless you. Thank you for being there for me. Your understanding of the Word of God is the bomb! Thank you for your God-given wisdom and all that you do for the people of God.

Rev. Carolyn Ferguson, what can I say? Another wonderful awesome women of God. All the classes you taught between 2007 and 2008 were God sent. It helped me tremendously to push past the fear to write this book. I thank God for your anointing and your gift of teaching and keeping it real!

Evangelist Zarlene McKinley, I thank God for you and your anointing. Thank you for being you!

I want to thank my two sisters in Christ: Awilda Labrador and Joyce Whaley. Thank you for praying for me and with me, your godly wisdom and advice that life has taught you both!

I thank my parents for teaching me about who God is. Your marriage and love for one another is a wonderful example for other couples. I thank my brothers for being there for me and always calling and checking on their little sister.

Chapter 1

Joy arrived at her job interview forty-five minutes early, so she sat in her car with the engine running to stay warm. Joy had on her thermal underwear, two layers of clothing on top of that, her down coat, her red hat, and her brown leather gloves. As she listened to a gospel radio station, and browsed through the recent issue of Essence magazine, she noticed that there was a public school nearby. Several big yellow school buses were parked along the curbside dropping off loud and talkative children. She watched the boys and girls dressed heavily in snow gear from head to toe walking and stomping their feet in attempts to knock off the melting snow stuck between the tread of their boots. All of a sudden she thought back and had a sad moment about her childhood and how she dreaded going to school in the mornings. It all began back at her Auntie Carmina's house.

Since Joy was the only girl in the family, she looked up to her female cousins because she wanted a big sister. She was eager to grow up. Carla and Cynthia Billings were about six or seven years older than Joy. Cynthia was the older of the two. She was intelligent, chubby, and wore ugly, nerdy glasses. Carla was slim and trim with long, flowing hair. They wore the latest styles in clothes, and it appeared as if they owned thousands of shoes. Joy often searched through their closet as if she was shopping at the thrift store and tried on every shoe that appealed to her.

There was a family get together at Auntie Carmina's house. Joy was having a good time as usual pretending to play dress up. She heard her name being called for dinner. She raced to the bathroom to change back into her clothes. Cynthia accompanied her and closed the door behind them. Joy looked around as if to say, *Okay why are we here?*

"Joy, lie on the floor, on your back."

She proceeded to do so, trying to figure out what was going on. Cynthia guided Joy, and placed her hands on her shoulders. Joy's pants were unzipped and Cynthia positioned herself on top of Joy. Joy thought to herself, *Is this a game?"* Joy focused on the peachy color of the bathroom walls and ceiling.

Joy said softly, "No, what are you doing?"

"Shh!" Cynthia responded.

Joy was distraught and confused. Tears slowly fell from her eyes. Cynthia tried to dry Joy's tears as they prepared to exit the bathroom door and enter the living room. Joy's heart raced a mile a minute as Cynthia extended her index finger to her lips saying, "Shh!"

After a while the weird exercise was over. Joy did not know what to think or say. She was in shock, her face emotionless. She acted as if this was the usual deal. They both walked out of the bathroom quietly.

Shaking her head and blinking her eyes to bring her back to reality, Joy took a deep breath. She closed her eyes and remembered her first day of kindergarten at the nearby public school. It's almost like it happened yesterday. As her mother exited the doors, Joy's big depressing eyes followed, wanting her to come back and make a run for it. Joy cried everyday for the month of September, and it continued for the rest of the school year on and off. Since these events came and went, her mother thought nothing of it. Her mother figured Joy would grow out of it, but this was just the beginning.

She waited in the warm, toasty car, she came to, and went inside for her interview. She said, *I'm happy I don't have those anxiety attacks anymore, thank God.*

The interview was a success. She started her part-time job next Friday after work. Throughout the day as she sat at her desk printing papers from her computer, Joy could not get her childhood out of her mind so she allowed her thoughts to go back.

Five years have passed. Joy was ten years old and everything seemed to be fine except each year for the first day of school, she bawled. It was like a ceremony or a ritual she went through every year. She attended St. Joseph's Catholic School, and the uniforms were the plaid blue and white oxford shirts. By now, one would think that a fifth grader would be use to the ritual of a new school year and not cry, but this spirit of fear and anxiety continues to live on within her. It's 8:00 a.m. and Joy leisurely placed her white ankle socks, boggy-woogy shoes, and the rest of her uniform on. She looked in the mirror and cried silently. She had no appetite, but she knew her mother would have her eat something. She dragged into the kitchen to meet her mom. Camilla, her mom, tried to encourage her to eat.

"Baby girl, are you hungry? You should at least have some toast or drink some juice."

She quietly responded, "No I'm okay. I'll just have a cup of water. Momma, I don't want to go to school today." Whimpering, she added, "I don't feel good."

"Joy, you said that all this week and today is Friday. What seems to be the problem honey?"

"I don't know," she said, shrugging her shoulders. "Can I stay home today?"

"No," answered Camilla. "You will be fine. Give me a hug and kiss. You be good and listen to your teacher. Okay?"

"Okay Momma." Joy's brothers walked into the kitchen, waiting on their sister to accompany her. She slowly walked to the door with her brothers, as tears gradually rolled down her face.

Billy, the eldest of the three children, yelled, "Come on Joy, let's go. I don't want to be late. Where is slow Alex?"

Alex the younger brother said hurriedly, "I have to put on my socks and shoes and grab something to eat. I'm almost ready."

"Joy what's wrong? Why are you crying?" questioned Alex.

Joy said to herself, If I knew, I would tell you.

She leisurely shook her head from east to west without saying a word. The more she talked, the more she would cry, and it sometimes got out of control, so remaining quiet was best.

They arrived at the school and saw all their friends had been playing outside before the bell rung. Billy consoled her, "Are you gonna be all right? 'Cause I wanna play kick ball."

She calmly said, "Yeah."

Alex followed. "Joy, are you sure? Because I wanna play too."

"Go ahead," she answered softly. "I'll be okay."

Joy opened the heavy doors to the school foyer and walked up three flights of stairs to the fifth grade classroom. The bell rang and the children's laughter and dread filled the halls. Boys and girls rushed into class hung up their jackets and then ran to their seats. Joy noticed all of her classmates and she gently smiled and waved as Ms. Willabrook stood front and center to get everyone's attention.

"Good morning!" the children responded. "Good morning, Ms. Willabrook!"

"I hope you all stayed busy during your summer vacation. Today we are going to let everyone present to the class what they did. Who wants to go first?"

Aaron quickly raised his hand.

"Okay, Aaron you go first."

Aaron traveled up front. Joy thought she was doing fine, but her heart raced, she was overcome with the jitters, and she felt woozy. She became exceedingly anxious and a knot developed in her stomach. Before raising her hand for permission to go to the restroom, a waterfall came rushing out all over the desk. The children shrieked at the puddles of vomit on the floor.

"Ooh yuck!

"Look at all the throw up! Don't get it on me!"

"That's nasty!"

Aaron yelled, "Wow!" What's wrong with her?" Others watched, quietly hoping that Joy is all right.

"Are you okay?" questioned Ms. Willabrook.

"Yeah, I need to go to the washroom."

"Sure," she said.

"And drink some water," Ms. Willabrook added.

"Okay, Ms. Willabrook."

Joy left the room with her head hanging low; however, her stomach felt so much better. She cleaned herself up, she was a totally different girl, she laughed and ran around, with her friends. The bell rang, and she grabbed her jacket and looked for her brothers in the hallway. They walked home, and everything was okay for now.

It was Tuesday and Camilla called for her children. "Get up Billy, Alex, and Joy, and shower. I don't want you to be late."

Joy went through the morning routine and came to the kitchen nicely dressed.

She began to cry silently. He father, Matthais, looked at her concerned, slightly raised his voice, "Girl, what is wrong with you now? Don't you start no crying. I don't care what's wrong. You still goin' to school."

Her mother placed a bowl of cereal on the kitchen table for Joy. She wiped her tears and tried to eat the Cheerios in front of her. She only took three mouthfuls and pushed the bowl away, afraid that she might throw it up if she ate more.

Every anxiety attack Joy experienced did not always involve her throwing up. She would always cry and try her best to avoid eating anything. But of course her parents were there to make sure she ate something.

Her family was somewhat spiritual, and they believed in God. St. Joseph's Church was where they worshipped. Her father did not understand the Catholic faith so he did not attend. Matthais eagerly searched the city of Evanston to find a place of worship but ended up empty-handed. Camilla found a service that had a broadcast on television with Pastor Carlton Arthurs from Wheaton, Illinois. He was an interesting man with an accent. Joy's mom got a kick out of watching and listening to this pastor. She was fascinated by his Belizean accent. Camilla enjoyed the ministry so much that she convinced her husband to visit the church.

On a hot summer day, the Jenkins drove two hours to Wheaton. Joy already felt sad in the car when they arrived. As the family strolled into the church, Joy began to cry. They all took a seat, and when they saw her tears, they had the usual expression. With concern and puzzlement on his face, Mr. Jenkins shook his head, wondering why his daughter continued to be so cheerless. The praise and worship went forth with the words on the monitor.

The choir director came front and center. He said, "Please join us to sing praises to our God. If you don't know the words, just follow the monitor. Hallelujah!" Everybody stood up, lifted their hands, and sang words to the song "I Need Thee Oh Lord."

Every single person in Joy's family sang the words except her. Sometimes she tried, but it didn't work for her. So she sat disgusted, waiting for the church service to end. During these bouts of high and mixed emotions, Joy was enthralled in her own world. She could never explain how she felt. Camilla was thrilled about the visit. She could not stop smiling or talking about the message. She tried to encourage Matthais to come back. "Oh honey, I really enjoyed the services, and I like the people. They are friendly, maybe we should join this church."

"Woman, are you crazy? I am not driving four hours to church every Sunday! That is out of the question. We have to find another one closer to home." Matthais searched for a church every Sunday. If one appeased him, he would give it a month or so. If not, he would visit a new church.

A community church was the next venture. This place of worship was nondenominational but reminded most people of a good old Baptist church. Once again Joy was dejected. She did not want to go to church this day. For some reason, she was nervous and felt like she had to vomit. She did not want to make a scene and embarrass herself and her family. The first time there, Joy entered the doors with tears again.

Her stomach was upset, and she vomited all over the carpet. Everyone looked around and questioned, what happened? But as usual, after the nervousness came out, Joy was brand new. She even participated in Sunday school and had a great time.

Joy was getting older, however, she remained to be anxious every school year, including high school. The life of a freshman was new with different experiences. Her family thought all of that anxiety stuff was over, but it was not. Joy tried her best to hide it so they wouldn't worry. She chose an all-girl Catholic high school, Queen of Peace, so she could participate in the Big Sister, Little Sister program. Her cousins Cynthia and Carla went to another all-girl school that did the same thing, and it sounded like so much fun to Joy. The seniors had to find a freshman to be their little sister. They would exchange numbers, write letters, and get to know one another. It was like a mentorship.

As the first day approached, Joy became nervous. She was sitting in the kitchen drinking a glass of water when the phone rang. It was her friend Trina with questions about school.

As Trina, the reporter in training, continued to ask these questions, Joy's mind began to race with "what ifs." *What if I can't make any friends? What if I have an attack?* Trina interrupts Joy's chaotic thoughts with a question, "Joy, are you there?"

"Yeah I'm here. Hold on for a minute." Joy dropped the phone and ran to the bathroom because she felt like she had to throw up. Joy thought to herself, *Is this happening again? I don't believe it. Why does this continue to happen to me?* Joy rushed to the phone with a frown as her eyes slowly welled up with tears.

"Hey Trina, I'm back."

"What happened?"

"I felt like I had to throw up."

"Are you sick?"

"No, I think I'm getting nervous about the first day of school.

Trina politely answers, "Oh really?"

"Yeah girl." Her voice shook as she tried to hold back the tears. "I've been going through this since I started school, and I don't know what is causing it."

"Well what do your parents say?"

"They are just as confused as I am."

"Well maybe you should seek some counseling." Trina always knew what to say and what type of advice to offer.

"Yeah I know. I'm tired of this, and I am ready for it to stop!"

Joy proceeded to make it through her freshman year, but continued to struggle with these anxieties. One day her father had a family meeting in the kitchen to see what would be in the best interest of Joy's well being.

"Camilla, I think our daughter should get some counseling so we can find out what's going on."

"Honey, you are right. But let's talk to Joy to see what she has to say."

Camilla yelled for her daughter, "Joy, could you come to the kitchen? Your father and I have been talking about those anxiety attacks, and we think it should be investigated by going to a therapist, but we wanted to know what do you think?"

Strolling in the kitchen, twisting and playing in her hair and pushing it back into a ponytail, Joy said, "I'm okay with it, because I am tired of this happening to me every year."

An appointment was made. Her parents picked Joy up from school and proceeded to the clinic. This clinic was in a nice area of Hyde Park, a quiet neighborhood with beautifully manicured lawns. Joy knew this was a step in the right direction to get the help she desperately needed. They walked through the sliding doors and stopped at the admissions desk.

Mr. Jenkins questioned the security guard, "How do we get to Dr. Jackson's office?"

"Go down the hall and make a left and you'll find the elevators. She is on the third floor."

"Thank you."

"You are welcome."

The family quietly rode the elevator hoping the visit with a professional would reveal some answers. Matthais and Camilla smiled at their daughter as they exited the elevator doors on the third floor. Walking to the receptionist desk, Matthais said, "We're here to see Dr. Jackson for my daughter Joy Jenkins at three p.m."

"Okay, said the receptionist, have a seat and fill out this form for your daughter's medical history." Camilla took out a pen, put on her glasses, and began filling it out. After twenty minutes, a young woman came out.

"Hello, I am Dr. Jackson," she said, holding her hand out to shake Mr. and Mrs. Jenkins' hand and then their daughter's.

"Follow me." She took them to a private room.

"Please have a seat," Dr. Jackson said. Looking at Joy's file, she says, "I see Joy has never been to a psychologist before."

"That's correct," answered her father.

The doctor said, "Joy, I am going to ask you some questions to see what's going on. What brings you here today?"

"I keep having these anxiety attacks, bouts of nervousness, every school year, and I don't want to eat. I get really nervous," explained Joy.

"Well, do you have any siblings?"

"Yes, two brothers."

"Oh. You are the only girl. How does that make you feel?"

"I sometimes feel left out because I'm the only one who doesn't have a roommate. You know, someone to talk to and laugh with."

As the session went on, the Jenkins looked at each other strangely, wondering, What is this lady talking about? That was the first and the last time Joy went to see a therapist as a child.

Chapter 2

It was Joy's sophomore year and her family was praying that Joy could deal with the anxiety better. This year she met a new girl who was friendly, petite, and wore glasses. Joy and Justine became friends when they joined the girls' basketball team. They would always talk during all the practices. One day Joy saw Justine, and she looked out of touch, as if she was not living in the present moment.

"Justine, what's wrong?"

"I don't want to talk about it."

"Okay," answered Joy. Joy was never one to force anyone to do something they didn't want to do, so she left it alone. Two weeks later after practice, Justine had that same look. She was holding back tears.

A concerned Joy asked her, "Is there something wrong? You don't look like yourself."

"I'll be okay, I'm just going through a little something."

"Okay, but if you need someone to talk to just let me know."

"Okay, Joy, thanks."

Three weeks later Joy saw a frustrated Justine. "Hey girl, what's up?"

Justine replied, "I really don't want to talk about it, but I have to."

"Okay," said Joy. "Tell me."

Justine whispered, "You can't tell anyone what I'm about to tell you, okay?"

Tears rolling down her cheeks, Justine said, "My mother's boyfriend has been molesting me for three years, and he is constantly bothering me. I don't want to be alone with him. How do I go about telling my mom? That's her boyfriend!"

"Oh my goodness, Justine. You have to tell her somehow."

"No! Are you crazy? She will never believe me."

"Justine, you don't know that. You have to tell a family member so he can be stopped. Are you at least going to see a counselor? You need to talk to a professional."

"I'm not ready. If I tell a professional, they may try to talk to my mom, and I'm not ready for that." She brushed off the conversation and said, "I'll be okay. Don't worry about me."

That was the last time Joy and Justine discussed that situation. The next day at school the bell rang, and Joy rushed down the hall to her locker. She saw Justine, and they spoke from afar, waving casually. Justine was still unhappy, keeping the silence within.

Joy tried to convince her to tell someone, but Justine tried to bury it, never to think about it ever again. Joy prayed for her that the silence would be broken and she would get the help she desperately needed.

During this time Joy became interested in dating. There were so many girls who had boyfriends or, in Joy's case, wanted one. This task could possibly be difficult to accomplish since she attended an all-girl high school. She delighted in movies about romance, friendship, and love relationships. All she could think about was the man of her dreams like she saw in all the movies.

It was the summer of 1988, the usual picnic season for family reunions and outside events. Joy's Aunt Carmina worked for the transit authority corporation, and they had a picnic every August. Joy remembered this day as if it was a story she read in a book. She never expected to meet anybody this day, but she did. Camilla and Joy pulled up to the center of the picnic grounds and unloaded the car. She spotted a small purple car with a young man sitting on the passenger side. Her arrival made her the center of his attention as he stared. She saw her auntie and greeted everyone.

"Hello everybody."

Her Auntie Carmina called Joy and said, "Joy, you have an admirer watching you."

"Where?"

"Over there in the car."

Joy looked and to her surprise, there was a cute young man about her age. She looked away and felt the butterflies in her stomach and the nervousness traveled from the top of her head to the soles of her feet. She went about her business and decided to play some games, like the potato sack race. She thought to herself and said, *Maybe I should ask this guy to join me in a game,* but of course she chickened out and changed her mind because she was shy and afraid of what may or may not happen.

This handsome young man continued to stare at Joy. Right before her eyes, this nameless fellow walked toward her Aunt Carmina. Joy looked intently from afar, and tried to figure out what would happen next. The conversation between Aunt Carmina and the young teenager flowed nicely from what Joy saw. All of a sudden, Carmina motioned her index finger towards Joy to come here. Joy nervously stumbled over as Carmina did the introduction.

"Joy, this is Lance. Lance, this is my niece, Joy."

Both teenagers hesitated and said nice to meet you. They both tried to say hello and successfully shook hands. Joy panicked because there was silence, so she hurriedly walked away! She thought of how cute this guy was. His cocoa brown skin was smooth, with no acne in sight. Joy's eyes focused closer to his mouth, observing his dusty looking mustache above his lips. Clean straight teeth were very important to Joy, and he passed the test.

The bright day soon turned to dusk, and Joy watched Lance walk to the water fountain. He bent over slowly trying to keep one eye on Joy and the other on the water, thinking to himself, *Will I ever see her again?* It was as if he was stalling, thirsting for a quick idea to connect with her just once more before leaving. Her eyes followed him as he walked over to the car climbed in and pulled off down the road. Joy was saddened by the fact that she and Lance did not exchange numbers. She started to daydream about what could have been: taking walks in the park, riding their bikes together, and even having Lance as a prom date. Joy literally made herself sick to her stomach. Day after day, she didn't eat. Her mind raced with crazy thoughts. She thought to herself, *It would be nice if I went to the store and saw Lance.* Six months later she called and questioned her Auntie Carmina. "Whatever happened to that cute guy, Lance, I met at the picnic?"

"Joy, you don't want to be bothered with him, he is a bad boy."

Joy responded, "Really, I guess everything happens for a reason."

It was another day after school and junior prom was coming up. Joy was doing her homework in the kitchen when the phone rang.

"Hey, Joy. What's up? How is it going?" questioned Trina.

"Oh, I'm okay. How are you?"

"I'm good. Hey, junior prom is coming up. Are you going to go?"

Joy responded, "Girl, I don't know. I don't have a boyfriend or even a guy in mind who would take me."

"I have a guy I want you to meet. He is Able's friend, Stan."

Able was Trina's boyfriend. They had known each other since birth. It was like they got the hook up in preschool. Since Trina was happy and in love she wanted her friend to experience the same, so they did a three-way call to Stan.

"Hey, Joy, hold on. I have to call Stan."

"Okay."

The phone rings.

"Joy, are you there? Yeah.

"Are you ready to meet Stan?"

"Yes, but I'm nervous."

"Joy, that's okay. It's natural to be nervous."

The phone rang once, twice then a young man with a deep voice answered the phone.

"Hello?"

"Stan, this is Trina. How are you?"

"I'm fine."

"Stan, I have my friend Joy on the phone.

"Hello, Joy, it is nice to meet you," Stan said.

"Okay, y'all talk!" screamed Trina.

"What?" questioned Joy in a shocked tone. "Trina, how do you expect us to talk while you are on the phone? Can we have some privacy?"

"Oh, I'm sorry. Sure."

"Stan and I will exchange numbers and call each other back."

"Okay, Joy, but you better call me later and tell me what happens."

"Will do."

Stan appeared to be more experienced than Joy when it came to dating. He had several female friends, but Joy did not allow that fact to bother her. The young couple talked on the phone several months before meeting in person. The Jenkins were in the kitchen eating dinner. Joy excitedly but hesitantly told her parents about her possible boyfriend to be.

"Mom and Dad, I have something to tell you."

Her father seriously answers, "What?"

"Well I have a new friend, and his name is Stan. Can he come over?"

"Around what time is this supposed to happen?"

"Dad, of course when everybody, or you and mom are here to meet him. Can he come Friday?"

Her father said, "I guess so. What do you think, honey?"

"That's fine with me," answered Camilla.

Joy hurriedly ran to the phone in the kitchen to call Stan. She picked up the phone and dialed. The phone rang and without giving him a chance to talk, "Stan can you come over Friday after four p.m. to meet my parents?"

"Sure, I will be there."

"Great!"

Immediately Joy became nervous even though she was excited. She thought to herself, *Oh no, I don't want to get anxious over such a happy event. What's going on with me?*

Friday slowly approached and Joy felt uneasy. Her stomach crawled into a knot and she did not feel like eating. It was horrible, but she made it through. It was 4:05 p.m. and Joy heard someone ring the doorbell.

"It must be Stan," she whispered.

She ran to the door and saw a tall, dark slender young man. He somewhat reminded her of Michael Jordan. He had a nice smile and beautiful white teeth to match.

Opening the door, "Hi, I'm Joy. Hello, I'm Stan. Nice to meet you." They both walked up the stairs to the kitchen door and entered. Joy's mom, Camilla was at the stove cooking fried chicken, mashed potatoes, and some collard greens.

"Mom, this is Stan."

"Hi, Stan."

"Hello, Mrs. Jenkins."

"Mom, is Dad in the living room?"

"Yes, he is watching TV."

"Come on, Stan. Let me introduce you to my dad."

They walked down the hallway to the living room.

"Dad, remember I told you that Stan would be coming over?

"Yeah."

"Here he is. Stan, meet my dad, Mr. Jenkins."

"Nice to meet you sir, uh Mr. Jenkins."

Both of them shook hands. Stan's visit was a success, and it was a plus that he was cute. The young couple continued the friendship for about a year or more.

Joy knew she wanted to participate in her senior prom. Perfect timing. Now Stan could be her prom date. One sunny afternoon Joy was in the kitchen eating a hot dog and doing her history homework when she took a break to call Stan.

"Yes, hello. May I speak to Stan?" It was a woman's voice. Joy assumed it was his mother.

The woman yelled, "Stan, telephone!"

"Okay," Stan called from a distance. Joy waited nervously and hoped Stan would escort her to the senior prom.

"Hello?"

"Hey, Stan. This is Joy. How are you?"

"Oh, I'm fine now since I'm talking to you!"

"You need to quit playing. What are you doing?"

"Nothing. Just chillin." Why? What's up?"

"Well, my senior prom is in May, and I was hoping you could accompany me!"

"Sure, no problem."

"Okay I'll call you later to give you all the details so we can figure out what color we are going to wear. Okay?"

"Cool. Talk to you later."

The prom was approaching quickly. They chose royal blue as their color. The day of prom Joy appeared to be content, happy, and cool as a cucumber, but inside there was a tornado of emotions roaring, waiting to come out.

After bathing, Joy went to her room to put on her dress. She couldn't decide whether to put her jewelry on first or her dress. Pacing back and forth, her body became numb and tingled. It was such a weird sensation. She was dazed, but continued to put on her pantyhose to push through the anxiety. Her stomach was empty, and she began to gag, looking for a garbage can to spit in. She was finally dressed, and she heard laughter and voices outside her bedroom door. Her extended family members were there to see her off. She slowly walked out into the kitchen like a princess, she smiled and hid her true emotions.

"Oh Joy, you are so beautiful! Turn around and let me see your hair! Ooh your hair is sharp, girl," said her overjoyed aunt. Joy decided to go to the extreme with her prom, so she chopped most of her hair off. It was like a Toni Braxton haircut but even shorter. It was sassy and perfect for such an event.

Bashfully she responded, "Thank you, auntie."

Joy's father took plenty of pictures. And before they could leave, her best friend Trina appeared with her boyfriend Abel. So of course more pictures were taken of both couples.

By this time, Joy was ready to go. So Stan opened the door, and Joy carefully climbed in the sleek black sports car. For some reason Joy was worried.

"Stan, what time is it?"

"It is six forty-five."

Stan tried to convince his date, they would not be late. "Joy, Abel has to stop by his mom's house so she can see us altogether."

Joy whispered to herself, *We do not have time for this. If we arrive at the prom late, they will not serve us dinner.* She rolled her eyes, huffed and puffed and mumbled under her breathe, "He's getting on my nerves."

After the quick stop, they were off to the Hyatt Regency in downtown Evanston. Finally they arrived, and Stan found a parking place. Joy was nervous, and she did not know why. As she climbed out of the car, she panicked. Her heart was beating a mile a minute. She couldn't swallow, and she felt sick to her stomach. She was walking with Stan, and then she stopped.

"Joy, what's wrong? Are you okay?"

"No. I don't feel good. I think I have to throw up." Stan gently fixed his hands on her waist and said, "You'll be fine. Let's go inside." Joy gulped down a handful of air and pushed tons of emotions behind.

They arrived just in time to dine. Everyone was sitting at the shiny decorated tables eating a variety of hors d' oeuvres, pizza slices, crackers and cheese and ham. Once Joy entered the building and saw her classmates, she began to calm down. Her stomach was still vibrating, so she was reluctant to eat. She nibbled on a small pizza slice.

The music was blaring. You could feel the bass in the floor. The song, "Make It Last Forever" by Keith Sweat was playing. Stan and Joy already had a great time together dancing earlier, but this time it is a slow jam.

"Joy, let's dance."

Joy said to herself, *He just wants to get close to me.*

"Okay," she said, agreeing.

Her heart was beating faster than lightning, as they held hands and walked toward the dance floor. She felt her body become warm as she moved closer to Stan. Stan was so warm. She didn't have to worry about getting cold with him embracing her. She settled her arms around his neck to get comfortable as he gently stationed his large hands on her hips. Stan was eleven inches taller than Joy, and soon her arms got tired. Her next move was to relax her arms around his waist.

Immediately one girl said, "Ooh, Joy, whatcha doing with your hands on his butt?"

Smiling, she replied, "They are not on his butt. My arms are tired, and this position is more comfortable for me!"

"Yeah right!"

Stan took it all in stride and said, "I don't mind. She can put her hands anywhere she wants to."

Other couples gathered around and hollered and made a scene, but Joy coasted in the moment. Queen of Peace senior prom was a memorable event for Joy. That anxiety was still a mystery, and she wanted to know why.

Chapter 3

By the early nineties, Mr. Jenkins still had the desire to find a church home for his family. Joy's father became very frustrated with the whole process until someone at work told him about the Church of Prayer. Joy's parents attended the church a couple of times before bringing the entire family. This church was like no other she attended. The church had thousands of members, and most of the people you saw looked well off. They wore fur coats and the best clothes money could buy. They drove to church in their BMWs and Mercedes Benzes. It was mindboggling. A lot of people, including Joy, could have been intimidated by the lifestyles of the members of the church, but after years of attending service after service and fi nally joining, she realized that everyone did not rock it like that. It was only a select few. One lady, Sister Doney, volunteered her time to the children's ministry. Sunday school classes were offered for children from the age of four to eighteen. Sister Doney was a no-nonsense type of woman who truly cared for the youth. She taught the four and five-year-olds during the first and second service upstairs.

After a magnificent worship service, Joy hung around to fellowship with some church members, and Sister Doney was one of them.

Sister Doney happily greeted Joy. "Praise Jesus! Sister Joy Jenkins, how are you?"

She warmly responded, "Oh, I'm fine."

Seriousness came over Sister Doney as she asked Joy a question, "Joy are you a part of any ministry because I've noticed you've been a benchwarmer for a mighty long time?"

She paused and became nervous and thought to herself, *What is Sister Doney up to?* Joy hesitantly answered, "Yeah you're right, I am a benchwarmer."

A benchwarmer could be a person who faithfully attended church every Sunday, but they have not committed themselves to a ministry in the church.

"Great. I have a wonderful opportunity for you. How would you like to assist me with the children's church?"

"What do I have to do?"

"You will assist me with the children. You know, pass out papers and snacks, whatever I need you to do."

"Okay, that sounds like a plan," Joy said.

"Meet me upstairs in Room 210 at eight a.m. You can watch to see if this is something you want to do."

"Okay, see you next Sunday."

Joy came to church at 8:00 a.m. sharp. *It's almost like a ghost town*, she whispered to herself, *Man, where is everybody?*

She bumped into a sister in the hallway and she inquiried, "Yes, can I help you? Who are you looking for?"

"I'm looking for Sister Doney. I'm supposed to work with her today."

"She'll be here shortly. Just wait for her in the room across the hall.

"Thanks."

She sat for ten minutes by herself in a pale blue room. There were several chairs and the walls were decorated with Scripture, such as "I will bless the Lord at all times; His praise shall continually be in my mouth" (Psalm 34:1 KJV).

People started strolling in, young adults and children of all ages.

Then she saw Sister Doney.

"Well, praise Jesus and good morning, Joy. You made it."

"Yes, I did."

"Everyone who works in the children's church meets here for prayer first," Sister Doney said. "Then after that we will go to my classroom."

Joy was impressed at all the children and young adults and their prayers. She said to herself, *Wow I wonder if I will ever be able to have a powerful prayer like that.*

Parents rushed their children to the door and dropped them off so they could speed back down to the sanctuary for the worship service. Forty-five minutes with these children was interesting, and since Joy was not a part of a ministry, she decided to make this one hers. It appeared to be easy and fun, and the children were so cute. She thought to herself, *Maybe these children can teach me something about the Bible because the Lord knows I am a babe in Christ.* Three months passed and Sister Doney was already trying to get Joy to teach a class by herself.

She encouraged Joy. "Girl, you will be teaching a class by yourself pretty soon."

She surprisingly answered, "What? I don't know about that."

"Why, Joy?"

"I'm not ready. I need more time."

"Okay," replied Sister Doney. "But you better get ready."

For some reason Joy did not feel comfortable. Even though she was an adult, she didn't feel like she had the knowledge and spiritual leadership skills to teach four and five-year-olds. Other teachers noticed Joy and would jokingly say, "Girl, soon you will be all by yourself teaching."

Joy would always respond, "Uh, uh. I'm not ready."

"Why," asked the teacher?"

"I don't know."

"What's wrong? You scared?"

"No," said Joy.

The other teacher Jenny said, "Girl, you cannot be afraid of the children."

Joy would listen and question herself, *Yeah, why am I so scared? What is there to fear?*

A year passed, and it was time for Joy to be on her own. It was almost like the first day of school. She was nervous, full of mixed emotions, anxiety, and a sprinkle of sadness. But as soon as she entered the doors of the classroom, she mellowed out. It was amazing. This baffled Joy, and she truly needed answers to these mysterious happenings. Even though she continued to teach every Sunday, there was fear, and she could not understand it or stop it from happening.

A year and a half passed, and she still was not use to teaching the kids. At this time, she began to have interest in other ministries, such as singing in the choir or the homeless ministry. She pondered and prayed.

What will the children's church do without me? They are always in need of someone's help. If I do leave, how will I say it and what will I say? Joy figured this would be a great opportunity to escape from the anxiety. Singing in the choir was a dream of hers, but she threw that thought to the side for now. Picking a career and university was her main focus.

Excitement of college sounded like so much fun. Joy wanted to experience campus life but was not ready with all of those anxieties. She chose Columbia College downtown and commuted for the first three years. While there she did not do her best. She did enough work and passed by the skin of her teeth. Initially her dream was to be a disc jockey, but after taking a few classes, she changed her mind. Her junior year was coming to an end, and she was labeled as a liberal arts major. Joy wanted a specific major, so she had to make a decision: stay at Columbia or go somewhere else and start over.

She really wanted to take a year off, work, and truly meditate on her purpose in life, but her parents would not let her. Now she felt it was time to experience college life away from home, so she went to Southern Illinois University, following in her cousin's footsteps. She majored in business.

During that summer of 1994, Joy wanted to be on top of things before she started SIU in the fall, so she took accounting II and physics. What a horrible mistake. She felt as if she was living in China. She had no clue what was going on in either class, plus the teachers were moving at an extremely fast pace. Joy was failing and dropped both classes. This was a warning for her, but did she listen? Of course not. She went down to SIU in August believing she would excel in business, but the opposite happened.

SIU was different from Columbia College. The professors did not appear to be approachable. Joy had seventy-four credit hours, and they basically made her start all over. She was like a sophomore. This was her first time ever away from home. Joy felt like an oddball at school. She had no friends except her roommate, who appeared to know everybody.

Sasha was a socialite, and she was not shy getting to know people. It took a while for Joy to make friends and to adjust. She stayed to herself a lot and in her room. She ate alone too. A part of Joy's problem was those anxieties. They held her back sometimes, especially to campus life, classes, and the professors. The classes were huge. Joy had to build up her confidence in getting to know the teachers. Some of them could be intimidating, but Joy learned how to communicate with them and not be afraid to ask questions.

Her first semester at SIU was rough holding down thirteen credit hours. Joy proceeded to tackle difficult math, accounting, and microeconomics. Her easiest and most fun class was ballet. Later on she thought maybe she should pursue dance, but of course she changed her mind. Her grades the first semester at SIU were horrible. She got an A in bal-let, but everything else was C's, D's, and F's. At most uni-versities, when a student's grade point average hits below average, they are put on academic probation. She qualified for a program to assist her. Joy was required to take a few classes on studying and how to bring up her grades the next semester. She was asked the question: "What do you want to do with your life?" She was tired and frustrated and looked for something easy and quick. Recreation sounded like a dif-ferent, interesting major. She thought to herself, *You don't have to do a lot of thinking with that.* But in the back of her mind, something continued to tell her communications or writing. So she chose broadcast journalism and felt like she found her calling.

Chapter 4

When she came home from school for the summer, she committed herself to become a faithful pew member at church, but did not offi cially get baptized. Her second year at SIU welcomed many new friends. These friends were Christians who decided to start their own Bible study. Throughout her four years at SIU, she continued to seek God intimately. She made it her business to attend church service as often as possible and to spend quality time with God and His Word in her room early in the morning.

As she continued to meet new Christians every day, she bumped into a middle-aged woman from the islands. This woman made it her business to minister to Joy. The two women had a serious talk about sins. The islanders' approach was odd, but she made her point. At the end of the conversation, Joy was crying. Joy knew it was time for her to give her life to God.

When Joy came home for spring break in March, she got up and walked down the aisle to get baptized at church. She was nervous but ready to take the next step in the right direction. She shed a few tears and knew this is what God wanted her to do at this time in her life. She was excited and ready for a fresh journey and how it would go. Spring break was over, and it was time to hit the books. Still suffering from anxieties, she found a counseling group of others who were violated or abused as children. In the first session she could not believe her ears, these students had it worse than Joy could ever imagine. Some were abused for several years, and it had only happened once to Joy. These sessions made Joy feel better.

Two years had passed and it was graduation time. She's thrilled and ready to take on the world and make some real money. It took her three months to find a job as a secretary. For some reason that summer she decided to have a serious talk with her mother about the violation. At this time Joy was not very happy. She was unhappy and felt alone. One day she walked into the kitchen and saw her mother reading at the table quietly.

"Mom, can I talk to you for a moment?"

"Sure, honey what's on your mind?"

Joy's face changed dramatically to a sad expression. Her eyes, shiny as tears, filled them. Her heart was racing, and she was unsure if she should go forward with revealing her secret. She thought to herself, *Will she believe me?* It was on Joy's heart to get this off her chest. She never thought in a million years that she would tell anyone what happened to her.

Hesitating, she said, "Uh, Mom I have something to tell you."

"Yes, dear, go ahead. Joy, why are you looking so troubled?"

She ignored her mother's question and said, "Mom when I was five years old, I was molested by Cynthia."

"Oh my goodness! When did this happen?" Tears fell from her face.

"At a family function." Joy nervously played with a small piece of paper in her hand. "Mom, why are you crying?"

"Because you are making me cry." Joy smiled and felt so much better. Camilla said, "I can't believe that Cynthia would do such a thing like that."

Joy continued to empty her heart of other events. "Mom, what happened to me? I did the same to three others when I was an adolescent, maybe between the ages of nine to eleven.

Camilla responded disgusted, "Oh Joy." Camilla could not believe her ears.

"Mom, I didn't mean to do it. It was not something I planned, it just happened. I asked God for forgiveness because I still feel bad for what I did. It was like a dream like I really wasn't doing it."

"Joy, do you want to tell your dad? He has to know too."

She whispered, "I know."

Two hours had passed, and she heard the rattle of keys in the back door. It was her happy-go-lucky father, Matthais. Joy was so scared. She felt like she would pee in her pants. Matthais greeted his wife, "Hey honey how ya doing today?" giving her a sweet peck on the lips.

"I'm fine."

"Hey, baby girl! What's going on? What you been up to?"

"Matthais, your daughter has something to tell you," Camilla said.

"What's wrong?"

With seriousness and a slight sadness in her eyes, she quietly whispered, "Dad, when I was five years old, Cynthia molested me in their bathroom."

"What?" was his reaction. His face was fully disgusted, with wrinkles all over his forehead. He couldn't believe it.

"Man! Umph." There was silence for a minute or two. He tried to encourage her after hearing such devastating news.

"A lot of kids go through things and they never tell. Honey, I'm glad you were able to tell us. Everything is going to be all right. Do you want to confront her and talk about this?"

She hurriedly said, "No! I don't want to." She wiped her face, drying her tears.

Her father, desperately looked for a solution to help his baby girl, and said, "Well what about making an appointment with the pastor or a minister at church?"

She quickly answered, "No! Not yet, maybe later." For some reason Joy felt like she would feel more comfortable speaking with a women about this ordeal.

A month passed, and Joy was feeling great. She later shared the news with her friend Trina. "Wow. What made you reveal the secret?" Trina asked.

"I really don't know. It's like God put it on my heart to just let it go, and I feel so good." Joy was hesitant to tell her friend because she thought she would judge her, but she didn't.

Some years after the violation, she did not feel comfortable hugging people, and she would always hesitate. *Should I or shouldn't I?* would run through her head. It opened up the door to her curiosity of what sex was all about. She found boys her age who liked to sneak and hide away. During this time it caused her to experiment with boys her age and "play house." It might have been wrong, but it felt good.

One day while sitting in the living room with her parents, her father was watching his favorite show, Judge Wapner in The People's Court. A pretty, young, lady walked into the courtroom. The announcer said, "She is suing her partner for one thousand dollars." The music played and entered her partner, a woman. Joy shockingly looked on to see what happened next. Joy questioned herself, *Is she a lesbian? Why is she so pretty? I thought lesbians were more manly looking.*

Her father interrupted her thought process. "That girl is too cute to be chasing after a woman!"

Joy said to herself, *Look at what happened to me and what I did? Is my cousin a lesbian? Am I a lesbian? No. I know I like boys and so does she.*

About a year later, there was a breakout of a new disease called AIDS HIV. People called it the homosexual disease because they were the main group of people falling ill. Every time the six o'clock news would come on, Joy would focus on the broadcast. *What kind of disease is this? Is it possible that I might have it or gotten it from somebody?*

Joy truly didn't understand, until more cases were found of children and drug addicts having the disease. One boy by the name of Ryan White even contracted AIDS through a drug he was prescribed to treat severe hemophilia.

This was a scary situation for Joy because she thought she might have contracted the disease. Later on she realized that wasn't the case but this epidemic caused her to refrain from sex period. She wasn't ready to be a parent and was not ready to die before her time.

As Camilla sat in her bedroom, all of this devastating news was bouncing around in her head. She didn't know what would be the next move in helping her daughter to get through this period in her life. Joyce Meyers, a pastor from St. Louis, Missouri wrote a book called *Beauty For Ashes:*

Emotional Healing. This woman experienced a grueling childhood by the hands of her father; nevertheless, God healed her and made her into the wonderful woman of God she has become. Camilla thought, *This is a perfect book for Joy, and I know it will help her.* She ordered the book and gave it to Joy when it came in the mail.

Receiving the book, Joy glanced at the author's name. "Joyce Meyer? Who is she?"

"She is someone who wrote a book about her life as a young girl. Please read the book. I know it will help you."

"Okay Mom, thanks," giving her a hug and a kiss on the cheek. She began to read it immediately as she exited her mother's bedroom. Her jaw dropped. She couldn't believe the words she read on the page. Joy read the book faithfully until she finished. It helped her tremendously with Scriptures and issues of abuse. It was an eye-opener for her.

Joy felt decent. She didn't realize that revealing a horrible secret could be such a wonderful sensation. It was 2003, and it had been four years since she made the announcement to her parents. Joy continued to seek God daily and to attend worship services. Every quarter the Sunday school offered specialized classes on specific subjects, such as, "How to Study the Bible" and "Who is God?"

One class caught her eye. It was called, "Let's Talk About It!" The facilitator was Dr. Lydia James. The following week on a Thursday the weather was nice and warm. Joy was looking forward to this class. She arrived at the sanctuary about fifteen minutes early. The church was always busy with activities on a weekly basis. She got on the elevator and rode to the third floor. The class started at 7:00 p.m. Strolling and looking for the room number, she heard soft melodious music floating in the air.

Upon arrival at the room, she saw a frail woman with long hair praising the Lord, lifting her hands, and worshipping God. Once she realized Joy was there, she stopped and said, "Take some time to get quiet before the Lord and worship Him." Joy really didn't know how to worship God or know what it really involved so she sat there quietly with her eyes closed. As the time grew closer to seven o'clock, more women filled the room. Later on, another woman came in that Joy had never seen before. She was short and brown skinned, with a big and bright glorious smile with eyes to match. This woman of God had an awesome understanding of the Bible and could break it down for anyone in layman's terms. The conversation was great. Everybody had something to say. A few of the women knew this woman and that she had a gift of prophecy. A participant in the class named Amber said, "You ladies need to listen to her. She knows what she is talking about. Everything she has told me has come to pass." Joy knew this class would be a part of her so called new ministry.

The following month, the prophetess came again to speak. Joy truly enjoyed the class and was learning a lot about herself and the Word of God. This time, the class discussion was about stories of different women who were sexually abused, raped, and violated. Joy grabbed and hung on every word the prophetess spoke as she painted a picture of each woman. The next thing you know something unexpected happened.

The prophetess said, "Myra was eight years old, and she was a loner. She didn't have many friends and she was shy. Myra's mother's boyfriend raped her violently for ten years." She stopped, gazed at Joy, and said, "Yours wasn't that bad now, was it?"

Shocked and a little confused, Joy responded, "No."

The prophetess continued, "I'm not all up in your Kool-Aid, this is God talking."

For some reason Joy felt like a little girl again. She thought to herself, *Uh oh, I'm in trouble. What's going on? I think something is going to happen.*

As the prophetess read from A Daily Walk In the Word, Joy listened intently at every word spoken:

> If you are a child of God, you have been infused with the same power that He "worked in Christ when He raised Him from the dead" (Ephesians 1:20 KJV). By His enabling power, you can forgive others with the very grace and forgiveness that you have received from God for your sins. Don't wait to feel like it or to figure out how it will all work out. Ultimately forgiveness is not an emotion. It is an act of your will–an act of faith. Don't harbor that bitterness for even one more day.

Fifteen minutes before the class was over, the women formed a circle with the prophetess. One by one, the prophetess spoke to each woman about their life. As Joy studied the conversations, she grew extremely nervous, she thought, *Oh my goodness, what will be said about me?* As her mouth became dry and her heart bolted, the prophetess looked at her and said, "You have some unresolved issues, and it is time to face them. You know what I'm talking about." That statement hit Joy like a ton of bricks. She made the connection of the women being violated and herself. She was shocked and surprised, forgetting that God knows all and He knew about Joy's past, her situation, and the years of pain, secrecy, suffering, and confusion.

After a powerful circle of prayer with the ladies, love was given with a hug. As Joy tightly hugged the prophetess, she cried loudly, releasing the pain and embracing the truth of her life. She could not stop crying. The prophetess said, "Here is my card. Call me if you need to talk." Joy took advantage of that offer. She called the minister at least twice a week, crying and asking for prayer.

A double load was lifted from Joy's emotions. This was the start of the healing journey, and it was a refreshing sensibility. Leaving the class for the evening with her friend Marjorie, Joy was still full and tearing up.

Marjorie said, "What's wrong Joy? Are you okay?"

Quietly taking a deep breath, she responded, "Yeah I'm okay. I'm really full right now."

The comment the prophetess made on Joy had her thinking. *Have I forgiven my cousin?* She felt she did because it was so long ago, and she tried to forget about it. She made an effort to speak to God in prayer about it to help her to move to forgiveness and to help forgive herself for any wrong she had committed. Joy felt as light as a feather. She had gotten a lot of issues off her chest and was ready to go forward with her renewed journey. Periodically she would meet someone new or come across an old friend while at the coffee house. Joy loved going to this place for a cup of coffee and her favorite dessert, carrot cake. Every Tuesday night was Joy time. She would bring books to read, or she would write, depending on how she felt. One day in deep thought, she glanced at the entrance of the coffee house and saw a middle-aged woman. She refocused back to her book. The petite woman with jet-black curly hair and reading glasses somewhat looked familiar to Joy. She continued to stare, trying to remember from where she knew this woman. The woman gazed at Joy as if she knew her too. The woman with the jet-black hair approached Joy. "Excuse me, do I know you from somewhere?"

Joy responded," I don't know. You look familiar to me too. Where do you work?"

"Currently I work at the post office, but some years ago I worked for the Yellow Cab Company."

"That's it!" said Joy. "I worked for the Yellow Cab Company too back in the summer of 2000. My name is Joy. What's yours?"

"My name is Marsha. Okay yeah, I remember you. You were the happy go lucky girl."

"Yeah that's me," said Joy. "Sit down and tell me what you been up to."

"Girl I am preparing to retire. And I cannot wait!"

"Really! How old are you?"

"I'm sixty-six."

"So what are you going to do?" questioned Joy.

"I'm going to travel, volunteer at my church and other nonprofit organizations."

"Okay, you seem to have it together." said Joy.

"Yes I do. And I also enjoy writing."

"Really? Me too. What do you want to write about?" questioned Joy.

"I want to write about my childhood and how I was violated."

"Wow! You won't believe this, but that's what I am doing now." exclaimed Joy.

"Girl, are you serious?" responded Marsha.

"Yes. Joy, I have experienced so much in life that needs to be shared. Other people need to be encouraged and to know life can be victorious. After seeing Marsha at the coffee shop everything came full circle and made sense. She realized God placed certain people in her life to take her to the next level spiritually.

One of Joy's favorite things to do was watch a movie at the show. She loved most of them: romantic, action-packed, and especially true life stories. This was a way for her to get away and escape her life temporarily.

Trina and Joy went to the theatre to see Tyler Perry's *Daddy's Little Girl*. Joy was known to be a bit emotional. She would usually cry at touching moments at the movies. This story ended happily ever after but in between there were sorrowful consequences. When Trina looked over at Joy she was crying, trying to dry her tears. Trina looked at her with disgust, waving her hand. "Oh my goodness, what are you crying for?"

"I don't know. I really enjoyed this movie."

"Are you okay?" questioned Trina.

"Yes, I am. Don't worry about me. You know I'm an emotional one."

Time and time again mostly every show she attended, crying would be the outcome. The last movie Joy and Trina saw was The *Secret Life of Bees* with Queen Latifah. Once again tears filled her eyes. Trina just didn't get it.

"Joy, I don't know why you are crying, the movie was not sad. From now on your name is May Boatwright."

"Don't call me that! That's not my name."

"I'm just kidding."

In the movie, May was one of the sisters of the Boatwright family. May was special. She would have these emotional breakdowns when she had gloomy thoughts. She would try to hum a happy song but then cry and run out of the room.

Joy had a few things going on in her life. She moved out of her parents' house and was on her own. It was very difficult for her. After a month, it had not sunk in yet. She described it as "sleeping over someone's house and returning home later."

As time progressed, she adjusted and really enjoyed her freedom and privacy. Within eleven months, it was time to make a decision, renew the lease or move. She seriously wanted to move because the management company was awful. The company had horrible housekeeping and allowed other tenants to do what they wanted, regardless of the conditions of their leases.

She began to shop for apartments and found one in the south suburbs of Chicago. Matteson was in a nice quiet area. The management company appeared to be friendly and professional, including the tenants. She agreed to bring a deposit of $150.

It felt swell to be on her own, and she was proud to say so. She was also afraid of failing and not being able to manage, but God was with her all the time. But somehow, as January approached, she got scared and a decision had to be made. She studied her bills and said, "I can't afford that apartment in Matteson, I'm going to call and get my money back." During this time her anxiety came back. She did not want to eat. Terrified she would vomit, she ate small portions of food to avoid that. With all of this came sadness and tears. After collecting her money, she prayed to God to give her direction. "Lord help me, I don't know what to do. I don't think I can afford this apartment. Strengthen me at this time. In Jesus' name, Amen."

Joy decided to ask her parents if she could move back home. She worried that her friends might ridicule her for moving back home, but she hoped it would allow her to save money. Her parents agreed that she could move home, but they wanted her to pay three hundred dollars in rent. Joy was upset.

"How am I supposed to afford that and save?" she asked.

"I don't know. You'll find a way," her dad said. "Are you still interested in our offer?"

"Yes, I am. I gotta go. I'll talk to you guys tomorrow."

Joy thought to herself, *Is my father crazy? He must think I'm rich.*

To make matters worse, Joy had no privacy or quiet time. There was always too much noise in the house. She thought, *Just to get peace and quiet, I may have to visit the library. Maybe I should've stayed at that ragged apartment building. Oh well, I'll just have to make this work.*

Prior to Joy moving back home, she continued to worry and have these very downcast moments that included tears. She didn't know if it was because of her monthly woman issues or something else. She made an appointment with Dr. Humphrey, a Christian therapist. She arrived at the therapist's office with concerned thoughts. *What if I see somebody I know? How will I respond? People might call me crazy for seeing a therapist. Man, I gotta stop it with these outrageous thoughts. Who cares? I have to do this to get healing and the answers I need.*

As she opened the glass door, nobody was in sight except for the young man vacuuming the carpet. She reached another door that led to a mini office. It was very confidential. It had a radio, a cream-colored sofa, and plenty of magazines. She casually took a seat and grabbed the health magazine. As she began to glance at the advertisements and articles, she heard someone talking. It was somewhat cloudy, and she could not decipher every word but knew a person was having their session. She thought to herself, *Lord, don't have me talking loud. I don't want the entire community to hear me.* After twenty minutes, it grew quiet. A gentleman with a briefcase came out.

Shortly thereafter, a Caucasian lady called, "Joy Jenkins? Come in, I am Dr. Humphrey. How are you?"

"I'm fine."

"Have a seat. Did you find the place okay?"

"Yeah."

"How did you choose me as a therapist? Did someone refer you or…?"

"Yes, my friend did."

"Oh okay. Let's get started. What brings you here?"

"I was molested by my cousin. This issue has been on my heart lately and was wondering could this event be causing me to have depressing situations." As she continued to speak, the tears came. "Lately I've been sad on and off. I figured I needed to talk to someone to get some answers to make sure I'm okay."

In the session Joy spoke candidly about her past. She said, "I feel my cousin learned this behavior. She was only maybe eleven years old. Where did she get this behavior from? Maybe someone else did the same to her. And it is a revolving cycle that continues until the silence is broken. The silence needs to be broken."

Joy wanted to confront her cousin and get answers of why she did it. She wondered how she should go about it. *Should I write a letter? Should I make a phone call, or should I do it in person?* The more she thought about it, the more nervous she became. It got to the point where the anxiety came back. She pondered all the issues involved, and she changed her mind.

She still wanted answers, so she went to the library to do research. She wondered, *Do children who have been molested suffer from anxiety issues?*

During one session, the therapist said, "Joy you are high-strung and very sensitive to your emotions. This can be innate."

Joy responded, "I was possibly born this way?"

"Yes."

The sessions continued until Joy felt stronger, better. At the next session, Joy decided to end it.

"Dr. Humphrey, I truly thank you for your time, but I would like this to be my last session."

"Okay," responded Dr. Humphrey. "I think you are doing much better, but if you need to talk, give me a call."

"I will," said Joy. "Thanks again. Bye."

Joy found a book called *What You Must Think of Me: Social Anxiety Disorder* by Emily Ford. Once Joy cracked open this book, she could not put it down. Joy could relate to the author and thought she had a condition, social anxiety disorder. The violation had to have made matters worse for Joy. Psychcentral.com explains repressing events:

> A repressed memory is the memory of a traumatic event unconsciously retained in the mind, where it is said to adversely affect conscious thought, desire, and action. Psychologists believe repression of traumatic experiences of sexual abuse is a defense mechanism which backfires. The unpleasant experience is forgotten but not forgiven which allegedly causes a myriad of psychological and physical problems from bulimia to insomnia to suicide.

Joy found herself living some of the same painful things, such as not living in the present moment but always thinking ahead and analyzing once the anxiety occurred. It interfered with everyday events, becoming independent by moving out, only to move back home with parents within a year, shutting down and secluding herself from family and friends and bad eating habits of not eating nothing or very little.

Joy wanted to make sure this was a correct diagnosis, so she went back to Dr. Humphrey's office. Joy brought her notepad just in case she needed to make a few notes.

"Dr. Humphrey, being that I am a curious person, I like to know the cause of things. Do I have social anxiety disorder?"

"No. A lot of these disorders are very similar. I noted that you have the adjustment disorder. This is a debilitating reaction usually lasting less than six months, to a stressful event or situation. Some stressful events may include starting a new job or conflicts with work colleagues. Some people who have recently experienced a stressor may be more sad or irritable than usual and feeling somewhat hopeless. Others become more nervous and worried like you, Joy."

Joy felt good leaving that session and had a hold of what was going on in her life ever since she was a little girl.

Joy was grateful for God healing her from all of the hurt and pain. She thought maybe she should confront her cousin, but only through email. She wanted to know if Cynthia would remember it, admit it, or even apologize. Joy had a feeling that Cynthia was also violated as a child. She emailed her, and it came back. Her next move was to write a letter. She mailed the letter and nothing happened. She doesn't know if she got it or what. She did her part and now, finally she can truly move on!

Through the years Joy has learned how to cope and deal with these negative, uneasy feelings. She developed a relationship with God, and He gave her peace. She learned how to worship and praise God in spirit and in truth, which is one of the best weapons against depression or any problem that may try to bind you or imprison your mind!

Bibliography

Johnson, Ophelia D. "Silence Broken: Surviving the Trauma of Childhood Incest." In Richmond Times- Dispatch (Richmond, VA), April 21, 1991.

The Daily Walk in the Word. Our Journey. Nancy Leigh Demoss.WITW.com, June 2009.

www.psychcentral.com/disorders/sx6.htm

www.psychnet-uk.com/ (accessed September 30, 2009).

Printed in the United States
by Baker & Taylor Publisher Services